JASON MIDDLEBOOK

LIGHT LINES

MILES
McENERY
GALLERY

511 West 22nd Street
New York NY 10011

515 West 22nd Street
New York NY 10011

525 West 22nd Street
New York NY 10011

520 West 21st Street
New York NY 10011

A CONVERSATION WITH THE WORK OF JASON MIDDLEBROOK

By Peter Heller

Eight Sunsets, I would like to have a word with you. If you have a second, I want to talk about love and beauty and home. A second is all you have, I know, because you are already slipping into twilight.

I remember running through woods the color of honey. I was seventeen. Early September and the birches and poplars, the beeches on Putney Mountain were already yellowing and the late sun poured through them and lit the world to amber. A few leaves had already fallen in the gusts of the last night's rain and they dappled the trail in scatterings of gold. And I remember the smell: the particular sweetness of turning leaves and damp earth and the cold stones of Sawyer Brook. It was a warm evening and I was wearing only shorts and I remember the feeling that the colors and the smells were coming through my skin.

I ran. I topped out at a rock ledge above a meadow and found myself looking east, across the hills and orchards and the Connecticut River to New Hampshire and the ridges there. I stopped and breathed and lost myself. Into the evening. There stood the lone peak of Mount Monadnock in the softest blue I had ever seen. It was not blue, it was a grained sea of translucent water and it lay over a flush that held hues of ember and rose that touched the rock shoulders of the mountain and deepened. And faded.

The sun had set over the ridge behind me and I shivered. Maybe it was that I was in love for the first time and I would see Margaret the next day; maybe it was that I knew my uncle and aunt and cousins were in the house three miles down the brook, maybe laying a fire in the woodstove against a clear cold night. Maybe it was the novel sense that I was home—in my body, in these woods.

But I remember feeling—or acknowledging—for the first time that I could bear the beauty...barely. That it was so immense, that the world was so full of wonder, that I did not know how to hold it. It was exquisite and it hurt. I did not know how to carry both the euphoria and the pain.

So when I approach you, *Eight Sunsets*, I understand your exuberance and also your bafflement. Your colors throb and fade as we watch, no power can still you. Memory has fractured you and still you come. You come in a dream in which there are corridors and passages that cannot contain you. You come reconstituted through the heart of a man who will cut down trees to carry you. Who will bring the scent of wood and lay it beneath you. Who will realign the grains of maple and walnut to reassure you of his commitment. Who cannot bear how much he loves you and is devastated by the love, and is lost.

You do not need any of it. Consciousness is a doubleness and you are singular. You burst off the wall and reassure us that you need no translation. That if memory comes in pieces, and passion with jagged edges of pain, you will throb and fade either way, and yield only to the first stars.

*

And so with the limb on its bed of green in *Spring Beauty*. Stand back and feel it as something alive that will reach for you from the wall.

Imagine: I am a tree. I am felled and milled. I am planed and cut to quadrilaterals on which, evidently, I am to be painted. But the shapes are refractory, they refuse to hold four sides, or easy angles, and they will not fit neatly.

And then: I *am* painted, a shade of AstroTurf, and scored with rulered lines like marks on an irrigated field seen from space. But guess what? The living limb cannot be contained. It surfaces and speaks to the original tree, the one beneath it. It stains the flat surround with a sinuous, irrepressible life. It taunts the artist and the viewer: you go through such effort to mediate me, to contain me in memory and reconstitute me in the studio of your imagination. You all do. My wildness frightens you. You will imprison me in city and plantation. But I will rise up, I will. I exist without you and I will live or not according to my nature.

And the moons across the room in *Three Moons, Three Nights* agree. They march through their phases and the light they shed refracts through the colors of a heart that is dumbstruck and can only beat on to its own music. There is nothing else to do.

All of art, if it is good and true, must enact this dance. It will reflect in every aspect the love that cannot be contained. It will hold awe and bewilderment in equal measure. And it might point with humor to its own limits. And so I thank the sunsets and the trees and the moons of Jason Middlebrook for reminding me what we're here for: to stand on a ledge at sunset and be overcome, and to not know if we should dance or grieve.

Peter Heller is the author of "The Guide," "The River," "Celine," "The Painter," and "The Dog Stars." He holds an MFA from the Iowa Writers' Workshop in Poetry and Fiction and lives in Denver, Colorado.

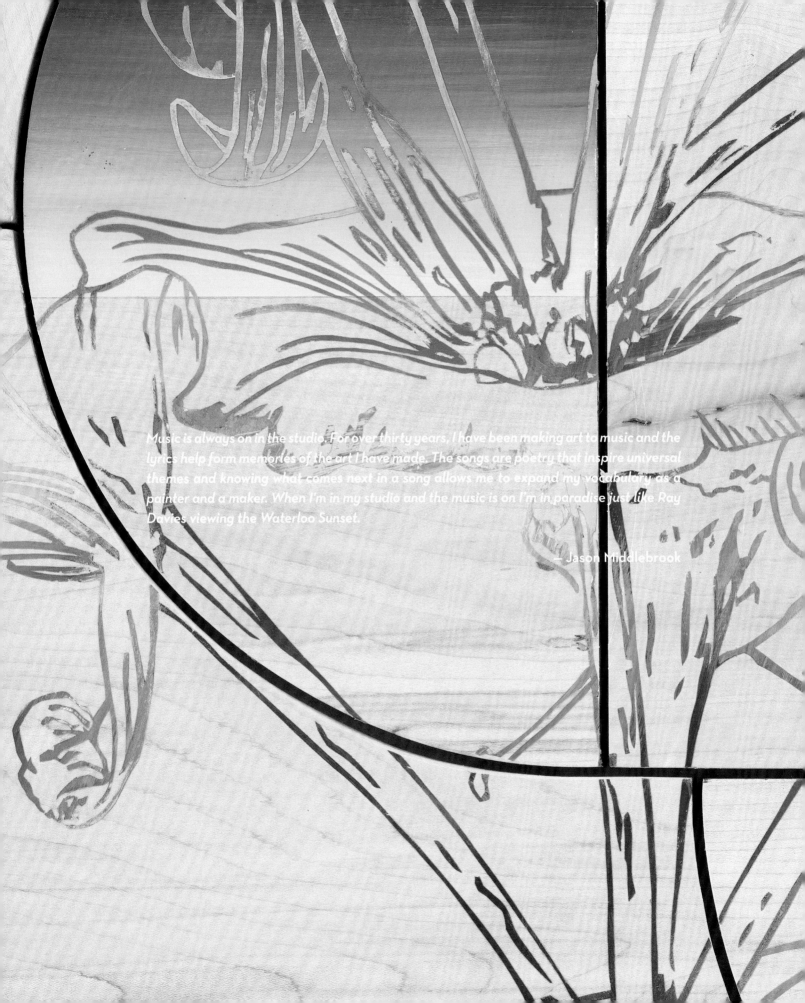

Music is always on in the studio. For over thirty years, I have been making art to music and the lyrics help form memories of the art I have made. The songs are poetry that inspire universal themes and knowing what comes next in a song allows me to expand my vocabulary as a painter and a maker. When I'm in my studio and the music is on I'm in paradise just like Ray Davies viewing the Waterloo Sunset.

— Jason Middlebrook

WATERLOO SUNSET

By The Kinks

Dirty old river, must you keep rolling
Flowing into the night?
People so busy, make me feel dizzy
Taxi light shines so bright

But I don't need no friends
As long as I gaze on
Waterloo sunset
I am in paradise

Every day I look at the world from my window
But chilly, chilly is the evening time
Waterloo sunset's fine (Waterloo sunset's fine)

Terry meets Julie
Waterloo station
Every Friday night
But I am so lazy, don't want to wander
I stay at home at night

But I don't feel afraid
As long as I gaze on
Waterloo sunset
I am in paradise

Every day I look at the world from my window
But chilly, chilly is the evening time
Waterloo sunset's fine (Waterloo sunset's fine)

Millions of people swarming like flies 'round
Waterloo underground
But Terry and Julie cross over the river
Where they feel safe and sound
And they don't need no friends
As long as they gaze on
Waterloo Sunset
They are in paradise

Waterloo sunset's fine (Waterloo sunset's fine)
Waterloo sunset's fine

— Raymond Douglas Davies

Altered View, 2022
Acrylic on elm
43 x 33 ½ x 3 inches
109.2 x 85.1 x 7.6 cm

Eight Sunsets, 2022
Acrylic on maple
45 ½ x 34 ½ x 2 inches
115.6 x 87.6 x 5.1 cm

Eleven Sunsets, 2022
Acrylic on cottonwood, maple and walnut
53 x 40 ⅞ x 2 inches
134.6 x 103.8 x 5.1 cm

Honeysuckle all the Time, 2022
Acrylic on curly maple
31 ¼ x 38 ¾ x 2 ¼ inches
79.4 x 98.4 x 5.7 cm

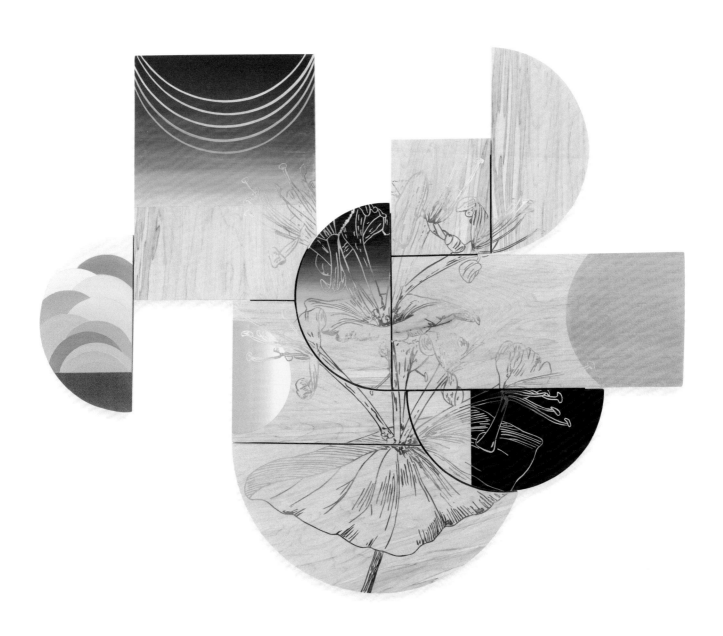

New Branches, 2022
Acrylic on maple, curly maple and elm
36 ³/₄ x 72 x 2 inches
93.3 x 182.9 x 5.1 cm

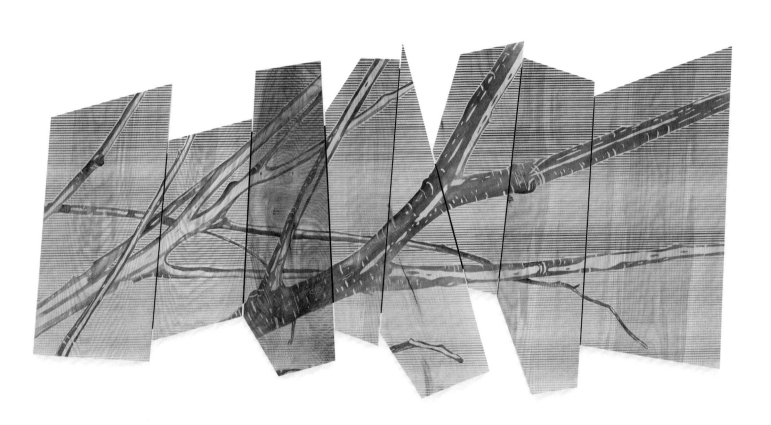

Night Chicory, 2022
Acrylic on elm
34 ½ x 25 ⅝ x 2 ¼ inches
87.6 x 65.1 x 5.7 cm

One Branch in Six Skies, 2022
Acrylic on walnut, cherry and maple
39 $\frac{1}{2}$ x 52 $\frac{1}{2}$ x 2 inches
100.3 x 133.4 x 5.1 cm

Road To The Top (Icebergs Are In Trouble), 2022
Acrylic on elm and ash
64 x 35 ½ x 1 inches
162.6 x 90.2 x 2.5 cm

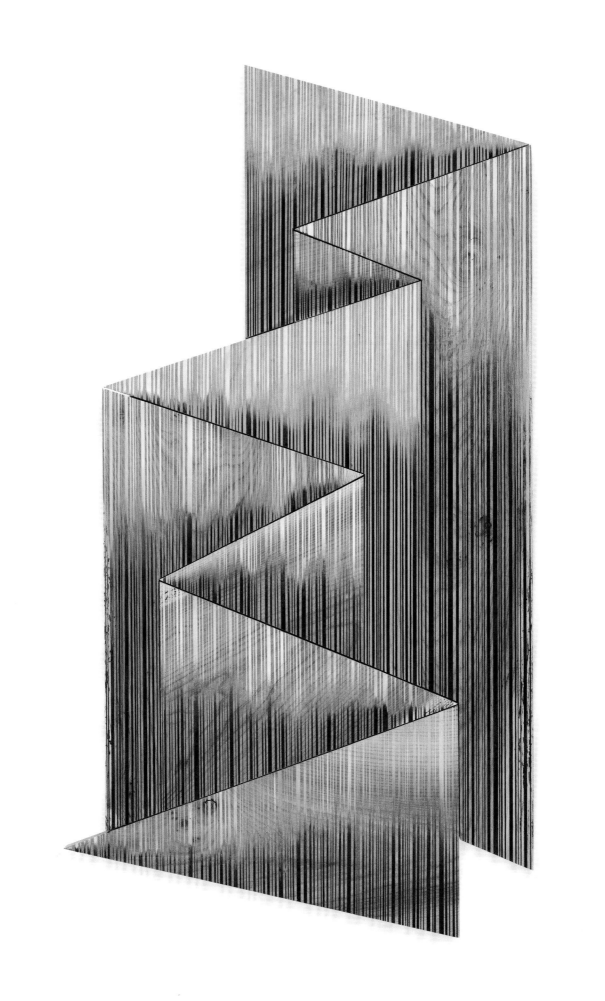

Spring Beauty, 2022
Acrylic on elm
66 x 37 x 1 inches
157.5 x 96.5 x 2.5 cm

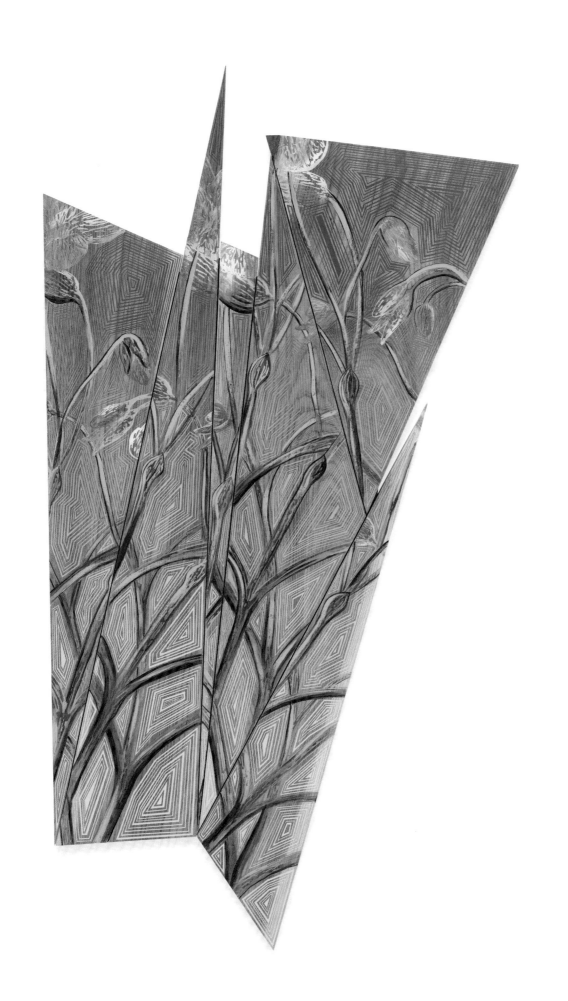

Sunset Cliffs, 2022
Acrylic on curly maple
38 x 40 x 2 ½ inches
96.5 x 101.6 x 6.4 cm

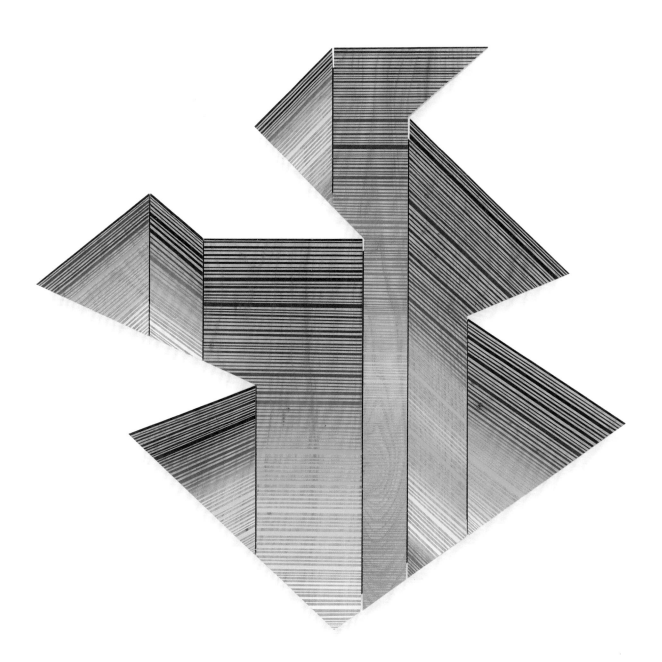

Ten Skies Towards Night, 2022
Acrylic on maple and walnut
29 ¼ x 25 ¾ x 2 ¾ inches
74.3 x 65.4 x 7 cm

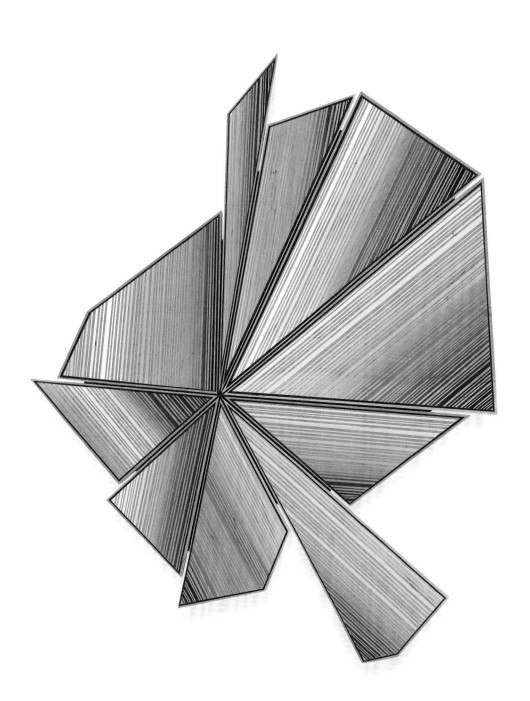

Three Moons, Three Nights, 2022
Acrylic on elm and maple
40 $\frac{3}{8}$ x 41 $\frac{1}{2}$ x 2 $\frac{1}{2}$ inches
102.6 x 105.4 x 6.4 cm

JASON MIDDLEBROOK

Born in Jackson, MI in 1966
Lives and works in Hudson, NY

EDUCATION

1995
ISP, Whitney Museum of American Art, New York, NY

1994
MFA, San Francisco Art Institute, San Francisco, CA

1990
BFA, University of California at Santa Cruz. Santa Cruz, CA

SOLO EXHIBITIONS

2022
"Light Lines," Miles McEnery Gallery, New York, NY
"Skies," David Smith Gallery, Denver, CO
Galleria Gianpaolo Abbondio, Piazza Giuseppe Garibaldi 7,
    Todi, Italy

2020
"Another World," Moss Arts Center, Virginia Polytechnic
    Institute and State University, Blackburg, VA

2019
Miles McEnery Gallery, New York, NY
Gallery 16, San Francisco, CA
LaMontagne Gallery, Boston, MA

2017
Jeff Bailey Gallery, Hudson, NY
"The Last Tree on the Planet," Lora Reynolds Gallery,
    Austin, TX

2016
"My Grain," Galleria Pack, Milan, Italy
"Drawing Time," David B. Smith Gallery, Denver, CO
"Time Compression Keeps Me Coming Back for More,"
    Lora Reynolds Gallery, Austin, TX
"The Small Spaces in Between," Gallery 16, San Francisco, CA

"Nature Builds/We Cover," Thomas Cole National Historic
    Site, Catskill, NY

2015
"Your General Store," New Mexico State University,
    Las Cruces, NM
"Gold Rush," Peters Projects, Santa Fe, NM
"Jason Middlebrook: Mosaic Tree Stumps," Jeff Bailey
    Gallery, Hudson, NY
Morgan Lehman Gallery, New York, NY

2014
"There Is A Map In Every Tree," Monique Meloche, Chicago, IL
"Line over Matter," Lora Reynolds Gallery, Austin, TX
"Submerged," SCAD Museum of Art, Savannah, GA

2013
"The Line That Divides Us," Lora Reynolds Gallery, Austin, TX
"My Landscape," Massachusetts Museum of Contemporary
    Art, North Adams, MA
"Underlife," Albright-Knox Gallery, Buffalo, NY

2011
"A Break from Content," DODGEgallery, New York, NY

2010
"More Art About Buildings and Food," Arthouse, Austin, TX
"LESS," Monique Meloche, Chicago, IL
"The Country Drawing Fair," The Big Draw at Wave Hill,
    The Drawing Center, New York, NY
"With the Grain," Galleri Charlotte Lund, Stockholm, Sweden

2009
"Live With Less," University Art Museum, Albany, New York, NY

2008
"Vein," Sara Meltzer Gallery, New York, NY

2007
"One Man's Trash is Another Man's Treasure," Kevin Bruk
    Gallery, Miami, FL
"Untitled (Let San Salvador inspire the way)," Museo de Arte
    de El Salvador, El Salvador
"Traveling Seeds" (commissioned by RxArt), Mount Sinai
    Hospital, New York, NY
"Jason Middlebrook: Disturbed Sites," Lisa Dent Gallery,
    San Francisco, CA

2006
"Live Building: The Recycling and Demolition of the
    Wurm Building," California Museum of Photography,
    Riverside, CA
"It's All So Black and White," Sara Meltzer Gallery,
    New York, NY
Galleria Paolo Bonzano, Artecontemporanea, Rome, Italy
"The Night Time is the Right Time," Galleri Charlotte Lund,
    Stockholm, Sweden

2005
"Alchemical Primordiality," Galleria Pack, Milan, Italy
"The Provider," Sara Meltzer Gallery, New York, NY
"Past, Present, Future," Margo Leavin Gallery, Los Angeles, CA

2004
"The Beginning of the End," Aldrich Contemporary Museum
    of Art, Ridgefield, CT
Aspen Art Museum, Aspen, CO

2003
"APL #1," Sara Meltzer Gallery, New York, NY
"APL #2," Els Hannape Underground, Athens, Greece
"Empire of Dirt," Palazzo Delle Papesse, Siena, Italy
Nylon Gallery, London, United Kingdom
Centro Arte Contemporanea, Siena, Italy

2001
"Dig," New Museum of Contemporary Art, New York, NY
"Museum Storage," Santa Monica Museum of Art,
    Santa Monica, CA
"Visible Entropy," Sara Meltzer Gallery, New York, NY
Euston Road Hoarding Project, Wellcome Trust, London,
    United Kingdom
210 Gallery Installation, Wellcome Trust, London,
    United Kingdom
"California is Still Falling Into the Ocean," Sara Meltzer
    Gallery, New York, NY

1999
"Subdivision," Steffany Martz Gallery, New York, NY
"Grand Entrance at the Commons," Public Art Fund of
    New York City, Metro Tech, New York, NY
"I Feel Like Making Love (Sempervirens)," Three Day
    Weekend, Los Angeles, CA
"Service Entrance," Steffany Martz Gallery, New York, NY

1996
"Real Estate," John Berggruen Gallery, San Francisco, CA

1995
"Identity Props," Arena, Brooklyn, NY

SELECT GROUP EXHIBITIONS

2019
"Arboreal," Moss Arts Center, Virginia Tech, Blacksburg, VA

2018
"Belief in Giants," Miles McEnery Gallery, New York, NY

2017
"Nuevas Adquisiciones: UAG Permanent Collection
    2015-2017," University Art Gallery, New Mexico State
    University, Las Cruces, NM
"Wood as Muse," The Art Complex Museum, Duxbury, MA
"Maker, Maker," Children's Museum of the Arts, New York, NY

2016
"Casa Futura Pietra," Parco Archeologico di Siponto,
    Siponto, Italy
"Geomagic: Art, Science, and the Zuhl Collection," New
    Mexico State University Art Gallery, Las Cruces, NM
"Craters of the Moon, A Project of The Sun Valley Center for
    the Arts," Sun Valley Center for the Arts, Ketchum, ID
"Beg, Steal, or Borrow: It's Nature that Takes the Blame," von
    Auersperg Gallery, Deerfield Academy, Deerfield, MA

2015
"Painting @ The Very Edge of Art," Contemporary Art
    Galleries, University of Connecticut, Storrs, CT
"Painting is Dead?!," Figure One, University of Illinois,
    Champaign, IL
"Misappropriations: New Acquisitions," Orange County
    Museum of Art, Newport Beach, CA
"Geometries of Difference: New Approaches to Ornament
    and Abstraction," Dorsky Museum of Art, State
    University of New York, New Paltz, NY

2014
"NOW-ISM: Abstraction Today," Pizzuti Collection,
    Columbus, OH
"My Landscape, abstracted," Museum of Fine Arts, Boston, MA

"SITElines," SITE Santa Fe, Santa Fe, NM
"Jason Middlebrook/Letha Wilson," Retrospective, Hudson, NY
"Painting: A Love Story," Contemporary Arts Museum
    Houston, Houston, TX

2013
"Second Nature," Albany International Airport, Albany, NY
"Eastern Standard," Greene County Council on the Arts,
    Catskill, NY
"Expanding the Field of Painting," Institute of Contemporary
    Art, Boston, MA
"Pattern: Follow the Rules," Broad Art Museum, East Lansing,
    MI, and Museum of Contemporary Art, Denver, CO

2012
"BAD FOR YOU," Shizaru Gallery, London, United Kingdom
"Left, Right and Center: Contemporary Art and the
    Challenges of Democracy," Gund Gallery, Gambier, OH
"Selections from the Collection," Museum of Fine Arts,
    Boston, MA

2011
"Beyond the Horizon," Deutsche Bank, New York, NY
"Feedback," Porter College Gallery, University of California
    at Santa Cruz, Santa Cruz, CA

2010
"Beam Board, Breath: An Investigation of Trees," Sun Valley
    Center for the Arts, Ketchum, ID
"Connectivity Lost" (curated by Ginger Gregg Duggan and
    Judith Hoos Fox), Zilkha Gallery, Wesleyan University
    Center for the Arts, Middleton, CT
"Alexander Calder and Contemporary Art: Form, Balance, Joy"
    (curated by Lynne Warren), Museum of Contemporary
    Art Chicago, Chicago, IL, traveled to Nasher Sculpture
    Center, Dallas, TX; Duke University, Durham, NC; and
    Orange County Museum of Art, Newport Beach, CA
"Think Pink" (curated by Beth Rudin DeWoody), Sarah
    Gavlak Gallery, West Palm Beach, FL

2009
"Lives of The Hudson," Tang Museum at Skidmore College,
    Saratoga Springs, NY

2008
"Something for Nothing" (curated by Dan Cameron),
    Contemporary Arts Center, New Orleans, LA

"Logan Collection" (curated by Mary-Kay Lombino),
    Frances Lehman Loeb Art Center at Vassar College,
    Poughkeepsie, NY
"Repositioning the Landscape" (curated by Jennifer
    McGregor), Westport Arts Center, Westport, CT

2007
"Collector's Choice III. Audacity in Art: Selected Works from
    Central Florida Collections," Orlando Museum of Art,
    Orlando, FL
"Sheldon Survey, An Invitational," Sheldon Memorial Art
    Gallery, University of Nebraska, Lincoln, NE
"Material Pursuits," Robert Hull Fleming Museum,
    Burlington, VT
"Craft in Contemporary Art" (curated by Evelyn C. Hankins),
    Robert Hull Fleming Museum, Burlington, VT
"Merit Badge 2," Rockland County Art Center, Rockland, NY
"Flow," Sheldon Memorial Art Gallery, University of
    Nebraska-Lincoln, Lincoln, NE
"Green Dreams," Kunstverein Wolfsburg, Wolfsburg, Germany
"Petroliana (Oil Patriotism)" (curated by Elena Sorokina),
    Second Moscow Biennale of Contemporary Art,
    Moscow, Russia

2006
"New York, Interrupted" (curated by Dan Cameron), PKM
    Gallery, Beijing, China
"Twice Drawn" (curated by Ian Berry), The Tang Teaching
    Museum and Art Gallery, Saratoga Springs, NY
"Inside/Outside: TreeLines" (curated by Amy Lipton),
    Abington Art Center, Jenkintown, PA
"Among the Trees," Visual Arts Center of New Jersey,
    Summit, NJ

2005
"The Obligation to Endure: Art and Ecology Since 'Silent
    Spring,'" New York Academy of Sciences, New York, NY
"Merit Badge" (organized by Jason Middlebrook), Hudson, NY
"Exhibition of Visual Art 2005" (curated by Dan Cameron),
    Limerick, Ireland

2004
"The Season," Galleria Pack, Milan, Italy
"Art on Paper 2004" (curated by Ron Platt), Weatherspoon Art
    Museum, University of North Carolina, Greensboro, NC
"Crude Oil Paintings" (curated by Elena Sorokina), White
    Columns, New York, NY

2003

"Paradise/Paradox," Castle Gallery, College of New Rochelle, New Rochelle, NY

"Yard: An exhibition about the private landscape that surrounds suburban domestic architecture" (curated by Robyn Donohue and Alyson Baker), Socrates Sculpture Park, Long Island City, NY

"On Paper: Masterworks from the Addison Collection," Addison Gallery of American Art, Andover, MA

"UnNaturally" (curated by Mary Kay Lombino), Contemporary Art Museum, University of South Florida, Tampa, FL, traveled to Kansas City, KS; Fisher Gallery, University of Southern California, Los Angeles, CA; Copia: The American Center for Wine, Foods and the Arts, Napa, CA and Lowe Art Museum, Coral Gables, FL

2002

"Majority Rules: Part One" (curated by Letha Wilson and Tara McDowell), Free Gallery, Glasgow, Scotland

"What Exit?," Paul Robeson Gallery, Rutgers University, Rutgers, NJ

"Sitelines," Addison Gallery of American Art, Phillips Academy, Andover, MA

2001

"The Altoids Collection," New Museum of Contemporary Art, New York, NY

"Wine, Women, and Wheels" (curated by Paul Ha), White Columns, New York, NY

2000

"La Ville / Le Jardin / La Mémoire" (curated by Hans Ulrich Obrist), L'Académie de France à Rome, Villa Medici, Rome, Italy

"Pastoral Pop!" (curated by Debra Singer), Whitney Museum of American Art at Philip Morris, New York, NY

"Never, Never Land" (curated by Omar Lopez Chahoud), Florida Atlantic University Gallery, Boca Raton, FL, traveled to Tampa Museum of Contemporary Art, Tampa, FL and Rutgers-Camden Center for the Arts, Camden, NJ

AWARDS AND RESIDENCIES

2013
Pollock-Krasner Foundation Grant, New York, NY

2012
The Workshop, San Francisco, CA

2010
Joan Mitchell Foundation Grant, New York, NY

2009
Iaspis Residency, The Swedish Arts Grants Committee's International Programme for Visual Artists, Stockholm, Sweden

SELECT COLLECTIONS

Addison Gallery of American Art, Andover, MA

Albright-Knox Art Gallery, Buffalo, NY

Altoids Collection, New York, NY

Denver Art Museum, Denver, CO

Harn Museum, University of Florida, Gainesville, FL

Marte Museum, San Salvador, El Salvador

Microsoft Corporate Art Collection, Redmond, WA

Museum of Contemporary Art, Chicago, IL

Museum of Modern Art, New York, NY

NASA Art Program, Washington, D.C.

New Museum, New York, NY

Pizzuti Collection, Columbus, OH

US Embassy, Podgorica, Montenegro

Whitney Museum of American Art, New York, NY

Published on the occasion of the exhibition

JASON MIDDLEBROOK
LIGHT LINES

9 June – 23 July 2022

Miles McEnery Gallery
525 West 22nd Street
New York NY 10011

tel +1 212 445 0051
www.milesmcenery.com

Publication © 2022 Miles McEnery Gallery
All rights reserved
Essay © 2022 Peter Heller
Lyrics © 1967 Abkco Music Inc., Warner Chappell Music, Inc

Director of Publications
Anastasija Jevtovic, New York, NY

Photography by
Christopher Burke Studio, Los Angeles, CA

Color separations by
Echelon, Los Angeles, CA

Catalogue designed by
McCall Associates, New York, NY

ISBN: 978-1-949327-78-6

Cover: *Spring Beauty*, (detail), 2022